*Dying to be Thin*

D1059866

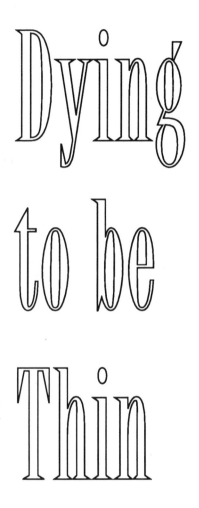

# Dying to be Thin

BY LINDA A. CARSON

*Dying to be Thin*
first published 1993 by
Scirocco Drama
An imprint of J. Gordon Shillingford Publishing Ltd.
© Copyright Linda A. Carson, 1993


Cover design by Terry Gallagher
Author photo by David Cooper
Printed and bound in Canada by Hignell Printing Ltd.

Canadian Cataloguing in Publication Data

Carson, Linda, 1958-
  Dying to be thin

A play

"Scirocco."
ISBN 0-9697261-3-9

I. Title.
PS8555.A77D9 1993   jC812'.54   C93-091752-9
PR9199.3.C37D9 1993




J. Gordon Shillingford Publishing Ltd.
P.O. Box 5269, Victoria, BC, V8R 6N4

# Acknowledgments

With the support of my parents and a close family friend, to whom I will always be thankful, my path went full circle and I arrived back to the place of my dreams, a place I had been forced to leave ten years earlier because of my bulimia. That place was theatre school. In the second year of the school I was given a challenging assignment. To graduate, everyone had to write and perform their own one-person show. I panicked. "Write?" I wasn't a writer! I was an actor! What would I write about? I liked a pirate character I had once played. A Pirate Show? I loved my Beauty Queen Clown, maybe I could write a comedy revue using her. Deadlines were looming as fast as my ideas were failing. I wanted to graduate! What could I write? "Linda! Write about something you know about," said one exasperated teacher. "Hmm," I thought, "there is this one thing in my life that I know a lot about…." And so began the process of writing my play, *Dying to be Thin*.

I'll never forget how frightened I was as my first audience gathered and I prepared to reveal my secret life as a bulimic. I'll never forget the relief I felt afterwards, and the rippling effect which evoked exciting discussion. It was this rippling effect that prompted me to continue to tell my story, in the hope that I would assist and prompt others to share their life stories too.

I want to thank my theatre school, Studio 58, for getting me started; Wendy Gorling and Pam Johnson for their ideas and support; and Carousel Theatre for taking the risk, and giving the play it's first professional production.

# Foreword

The assignment should have been routine: cover the opening of a new resource centre dealing with eating disorders, write a few inches and move on to the next story.

But that assignment for the *Vancouver Sun* in the spring of 1992 was the beginning of a remarkable journey, a journey that unfolded in stories of pain and triumph and survival. When I read that ten percent of patients suffering from the self-imposed starvation syndrome called anorexia nervosa die, even with treatment, I knew that I had a responsibility as a journalist to write about the victims of these disorders. As a survivor of anorexia and the binge-and-purge disorder bulimia, I could not turn my back on those who were not so fortunate.

In the weeks after my initial story, I encountered and profiled half a dozen young women who were willing to reveal their personal struggles with eating disorders in the hope that others could be educated and — perhaps — helped.

Some were still struggling with the personal demons and social pressures that caused them to starve themselves or binge and purge until their bodies were ravaged and their lives in chaos. Others had made the painful transition to a healthy body image and more normal eating habits, and hoped their stories would educate and inspire other victims and potential victims, especially young women.

One of these survivors was Linda Carson, a bouyant and versatile performer and writer who somehow managed to care for a new baby and wrestle an autobiographical script into shape without ever losing her composure or contagious good cheer. I was invited to a reading of her new play, *Dying to be Thin*, at the suggestion of Cynthia Johnston of the Eating Disorder Resource Centre of British Columbia.

The energy in the Cartwright Gallery on Granville Island that dazzling summer day was electric. As a theatre critic, first at the *Ottawa Citizen* and now at the *Sun*, I was usually excluded from the play development process, invited only to opening night performances of finished productions.

But that first reading was as exciting as any opening I've attended. Linda's script was funny and sad and wise and horrifying. We laughed as she talked about her techniques for making the scales lie during one of her twenty-four daily weigh-ins, cringed as she shared her tips for ending a binge with red licorice and shuddered as she described the horror of vomiting in a filthy public toilet. When she lifted her childlike face and confessed, "I don't know why I do this," we all shared the character's pain and applauded Linda's bravery for putting so much of her own life in this script.

Ironically, I never saw a finished production of *Dying to be Thin*, or got to observe students' reactions and questions at the post-performance discussions that were part of Carousel Theatre tour. But I will always remember the play as it was in that fragile, tentative but compelling draft, read by a woman with the guts and insight to bring her story to life on-stage.

There are some happy endings in this tale. My series was nominated for a British Columbia Newspaper Award, and Linda's play enjoyed a successful tour. One of the young women featured in the *Vancouver Sun* series is making a remarkable recovery from anorexia, and has reached a healthy body weight after a six-year battle in which her weight was as low as forty-seven pounds. Another has toughed out the waiting list and started programs to deal with her alcoholism and bulimia.

But for every man or woman who survives eating disorders or receives adequate treatment, there are dozens living with this secret shame or waiting desperately for proper medical attention. Adults with eating disorders in B.C. can wait up to two years for a medical assessment, with a further wait for actual treatment. The taxpayer tab for treating a single eating disorder patient in hospital can add up to hundreds of thousands of dollars.

Doctors, counsellors and eating disorder survivors now realize that one of the keys to breaking this self-destructive cycle is education and early intervention. The more information we can give teenagers, particularly teenage girls, about the dangers of dieting and the consequences of using food as a substitute for honest emotional expression, the greater their chances of escaping this deadly trap.

*Dying to be Thin* is a valuable part of this education process, as well as a dynamic piece of theatre. For eating disorder survivors, it is a testament to survival. For those who are lucky enough to have escaped this nightmare, it is an insightful and gripping experience.

Barbara Crook

## Production Credits

*Dying to be Thin* was first staged by Carousel Theatre, Vancouver, on November 10, 1992, with the following cast:

AMANDA Jones   Linda A. Carson

Directed by Pam Johnson
Set design by Douglas Welch
Stage Manager: Eileen Stanley
Production Manager: Bruce Watson
Sound design: Greg Sawka
Props construction: Valerie Arntzen

Character

AMANDA Jones (17)


Time

The present


Setting

AMANDA's bedroom. Occasionally the script will mention items like a
bed or chest of drawers but these are not necessary and can be
substituted. There does need to be some sort of table, a place or places
to hide food, a working toaster oven, a wall or bulletin board, and
something to represent a toilet.

# Act One

*(It is morning. AMANDA is lying on her bed asleep. She is dressed in her dressing gown. There are half eaten bits of junk food all around her spilling out of a paper bag. A tape quietly begins to drone: "chocolate, icing, cookies, bread, sugar, butter, cake, chocolate, icing, cookies, bread, sugar, etc." She wakes and looks at the leftovers. She feels sick. She listens to the drone; as if the words are the thoughts in her head. Heaving herself up, she walks to the bathroom. She looks at herself in a mirror, questioning silently why this person would eat so much. She then turns to the toilet. She takes a deep breath as the "drone" fades into the sound of constant toilet flushing. AMANDA begins to throw up a coloured, magician's streamer from her mouth. Finishing, she stands up and breathes a sigh of relief. The mirror reflects back to her a cleansed, more positive person, fresh for a new start. She leaves her bathroom, but as she does, she discovers the audience staring at her. Acknowledging them, she realizes that she has been caught. As the play continues she talks directly to the audience.)*

AMANDA: You, just saw that…. *(She makes an excuse.)* I couldn't help
it. I've got the flu…

> *(She remembers the spilled leftovers and goes to hide
> them in the paper bag but stops, realizing it is too late.
> She turns back to the audience and ensures them em-
> phatically.)*

…that was my last time.

> *(She goes over to her desk and pulls out her journal. She
> writes:)*

"A New Beginning."

> *(She stops and decides to confide in the people watching her.)*

I've had so many "New Beginnings"! Maybe I'm addicted to

"New Beginnings" and that's why I keep on blowing it. I am sick of blowing it!

*(She leafs through the journal.)*

I blew it here—and here—and here—here, here, and…. I'd die if anybody I actually knew ever found out.

*(She pauses and is suddenly hit by a thought.)*

What if I did die? What if—somehow—I ceased to exist and my Mom and Dad—or my friends read this? Woe!

*(She quickly rips out the previous pages of her journal and destroys them.)*

No way! No, no, no way!

*(There is not much of the journal left. After considering it, she throws away the whole book and digs out a brand new journal. She continues with conviction.)*

This book shall only contain perfection.

*(She titles it.)*

"Amanda Jones." That's me. "My Success Journal."

*(AMANDA closes the book and swears on it.)*

From now on, everything I write in this diary, will be a record of my success. "White Rabbits, White Rabbits, White Rabbits."

That's what my Grandmother used to say on the first day of every month. She said it brought her a present but I use it for good luck.

*(AMANDA is reminded of her grandmother's ring and pulls out a special box.)*

This is my Grandmother's ring.

*(She opens the box.)*

She gave it to me last year just before she died. I swore that when it was on my finger, my hand would stay away from all junk food, but I kept on blowing it so I put it away until I had smartened up.

"I hereby vow, on my Grandmother's ring, that I will be perfect from now on."

*(She ceremoniously puts on the ring.)*

Because…"diamonds are forever! And today is the first day of the rest of…forever!" I just have…
Twelve hours ahead,
A safe pathway I'll tread,
Before I'm safely back to bed,
Perfect living, all day long,
Surroundeth me!"

*(She finishes with one more, very serious vow.)*

If I ever blow it again—this ring gets flushed down the toilet.

*(AMANDA pauses and wonders what to do next. She looks around her room until she catches her image in the mirror. Her spirits slip a little as she looks at herself and she goes over to the scales. She takes off her dressing gown and carefully steps on. They give her worse news than the mirror and she gets off defeated. She remembers her vows and rallies herself onward.)*

Okay, okay, I just need to find a new diet.

*(She goes to a large pad of paper hanging up in her room and pulls down an old diet plan. She begins working on a new one. She writes in big letters:)*

"To lose! Ten pounds!"

*(Finishing, she imagines herself already there.)*

You know, right now, if I was ten pounds less? I'd be dressed in those Levi's…

*(She points to a tiny pair of jeans hung up on display.)*

…with my brown belt, and that white shirt tucked in—and

I'd have my homework easily done and slung over my shoulder as I breezed out that door to meet Robbie, he's my boyfriend, and we'd go and shoot some baskets or something, and then he'd walk me to my locker, and my friends would gather round and we'd all go into class, laughing.

*(AMANDA catches sight of herself in the mirror and is brought back to reality. She covers herself up in her dressing gown again.)*

If! If I was ten pounds less!

*(AMANDA sees a picture of her sister.)*

My sister is! This is a picture of her she sent to me from her university.

*(She reads the back of the picture.)*

"Dear Amanda, I hope you're felling better and that your new diet is going well." We used to diet together. "As you can see I finally managed to lose that last eight pounds and I'm *so* much happier and I'm having *so* much fun. But I'll be home next weekend so we can catch up. Love, April." I can't stand the thought of my sister seeing me like this!

*(Her spirits have slipped even further but then she suddenly gets excited.)*

Maybe this is just what I need! April coming home will make me really stick to a diet! I'll make up a "Sister Coming Home Plan!" One that will get me skinny by the time that she gets here!

*(AMANDA madly begins to look through a pile of magazines and diet books. She comes across a lovely dessert and shows it to the audience.)*

You know, sometimes when I try to diet, all that comes into my mind are pictures of these terribly fattening foods. And it happens when I eat too. I go to eat something that's good for me, like an apple or a carrot, and the next thing I know I am cleaning out the whole fridge. Eating's the problem! If I didn't have to eat—anything—ever—I'd be fine!

*(She suddenly gets an idea.)*

That's it! I won't eat! I won't eat until my sister comes home!

*(AMANDA goes over to her hanging paper and writes.)*

"Eat Zero Calories."

*(Very pleased, on top of the world again, she starts to get dressed while figuring out the logistics of her new plan.)*

It will be tricky with Mom and Dad. There's no way they'd let me do it. No way! My Mom swears by the Jenny Craig diet, and my Dad—he thinks maybe if I just don't eat between meals. So I'll have to pretend that everything is fine and I just can't make it home for dinner. I'll say—there's this big volleyball tournament coming up so we have to practice—but instead I'll just go for a jog by myself. Jogging! That's a great idea!

*(AMANDA goes back to her plan and writes:)*

"Jog!—One Hour Per Night." That way I'll burn up seven hundred and eighty more calories besides the zero I've eaten! I bet you I'll lose more than ten pounds!

*(AMANDA surveys her plan happily and decides to add: "Starting Weight." She then goes over to the scales and carefully gets on.)*

I weigh myself a lot. Probably—well, at least twenty-four times a day. If I'm on a diet I like to see the weight go down, and if I'm not, I've got to make sure the fat isn't sneaking back on—which it does! It's best not to wear anything at all though because every little bit adds up. I used to make myself strip down to nothing every time, even at school, but that was hard so then I weighed all my clothes, and now I just subtract them from the total.

*(AMANDA does a calculation and writes her weight up on the paper. If she wants she can add a heading: "End Weight" for inspiration, and draw a graph line down to her ideal weight of one hundred and five pounds.)*

I never use those big doctors scales, no way! They're good

for an instant five pound gain! I always use the cheapest scales going.

*(AMANDA displays her scales and demonstrates with them.)*

The cheaper the scales, the less you weigh—especially if you put them on a carpet! And I never jump on. I hold on to something and ease my weight on bit, by bit, by bit, so it ends up at the lightest weight possible.

*(AMANDA has held onto her table and is taking her fingers off one by one.)*

And if I'm not happy with that, I set the little marker to just below zero, and as long as I come off the scales super slowly too, it ends up back on zero so I can believe the weight I just saw!

*(She puts the scales back to their original spot.)*

It won't be long before I'm back in this bed tonight and I am soooo happy that I made it through my day, and I am soooo happy that I am skinnier!

*(She relaxes into the happy thought but then sees her leftover junk food and jumps back into her planning mode.)*

I've got to get these out of the house so nothing tempts me! You know, it'll be easier if I get *me* out of the house. The safest place is at school—but I hate anyone seeing me like this. Never mind, it's for the best and it won't be for long.

*(AMANDA makes a phone call. She has a phone with a monitor so the audience can hear the other party.)*

"Hi, Robbie here! SSSZZZZZZZZZZ. If it's before 8:55, I'm not up yet! Snorrrrrrre! But talk to me anyway and I'll get back to you."

*(AMANDA picks up the phone and leaves her message.)*

"Hi, Robbie? It's me—uh—listen, sorry I didn't get back to

you all week — I, uh, had this really bad flu — but I'm feeling way better today so I thought I'd come to school and maybe you could meet me at my locker and I could give you back your math notes and we could talk — and stuff. Listen, Robbie, my face is still really fat and swollen from being sick — I hope you don't mind.... Anyway, I'll see you in forty-five minutes. Oh, it's me — Amanda."

*(AMANDA hangs up the phone and gets herself ready for school.)*

My friends must think it's weird the way I'm sick so much. I used to do everything with them but now I'm always waiting until I'm skinnier before I let myself go out. Even Robbie's almost given up on me. We've been going out for about a year now. We run together, ski together, play basketball, volleyball...except this year I didn't even try out for volleyball because I looked way too fat in my shorts. I got so depressed I blew it for a week.

*(Ready for school, AMANDA gets the bag of leftovers and goes to leave but is stopped by a note slipped half way under her door. She picks it up.)*

"My dear Mandy, I didn't want to disturb you this morning as I heard you up studying well past midnight." I wasn't exactly studying. "Here is a snack to pop in your bag to feed your mind! We'll see you for dinner. Love, Mom."

*(AMANDA discovers some rice cakes left by her mother. She looks at them and then crumples up the note. Her spirits have slipped.)*

Doesn't she know that it's dangerous to let anything into your mouth when you first start out on a diet because you always end up wanting more?

*(She looks at the rice cakes.)*

The trouble is I am awfully hungry. I sort of haven't let anything stay down since — the day before yesterday. It's probably stupid to try to start off a fast already hungry. Maybe I should have one — to make up for yesterday. I mean, one rice cake in seven days isn't going to hurt anything! OK,

Mom, I'll have one.

*(AMANDA takes out a cracker and goes to eat it.)*

You know, since this is my last meal, I might as well enjoy it.

*(She goes to retrieve some peanut butter from a hidden spot.)*

Peanut butter. It's good protein. It will feed my mind!

*(She finds a hidden knife and spreads peanut butter on the rice cracker. As she finishes she gets another idea.)*

And you know what else? This will be delicious!

*(She dives to another hidden spot.)*

Chocolate sauce!

*(She takes a moment to justify it.)*

That will take care of my chocolate cravings for the seven days too!

*(She scoops on chocolate sauce. Her spirits have picked up again.)*

It looks like a giant Reese's Pieces! Except it needs a little colour—I have just the thing!

*(She gets some hidden Smarties.)*

Smarties! "When you eat your Smarties do you eat the red ones last? Do you suck them very slowly, or crunch them very fast!"

*(She covers the rice cracker with Smarties and takes a big bite, enjoying it. She takes another bite but suddenly stops and looks at the smothered piece of food.)*

What am I doing?

*(AMANDA drops the cracker.)*

Stupid! Stupid fat me! Some first fast! Why didn't I just get out of the house? Stupid Mom! I wish she'd just mind her own business! I'm such a moron! How am I supposed to lose ten pounds in time for my stupid sister coming home?

*(She jumps on to scales.)*

I'm already up a good five!

*(AMANDA eyes the gooey rice cracker.)*

There's no way I can let *that* stay down.

*(She continues, defeated.)*

I should have got rid of those Smarties last night—and that, and that….

*(She indicates the other food on the table.)*

I need to get rid of it all so it doesn't come sneaking up on me.

*(AMANDA pauses as an idea dawns on her.)*

Well, maybe that's it!

*(She begins to plan.)*

Since I have to throw up anyway—I could get rid of all my cravings and all this food at once! I could have this huge feast—of everything I've ever wanted to eat so that I'll never crave again! I can't believe I haven't thought of this before! I will have my—"Last Ever in My Whole Life Binge!"

*(AMANDA is feeling more and more excited. She retrieves her bag of leftovers that she was going to throw out.)*

It'll be good not to waste these!

*(She reaches into the bag and pulls out one or two half-eaten items and then stops as she finds some sliced, white Wonder Bread.)*

This, I love! Wonder Bread! When we were little we used to make it up into little dough balls.

*(She squishes some up into a little ball.)*

*Linda A. Carson*

It would taste just like home-made bread.

*(She eats it.)*

Mmm—dough-dough bread!

*(During the following section each time she mentions a food it gets retrieved from a hidden spot in her room and put on the table.)*

And these!

*(She has suddenly remembered another one of her favourites.)*

Pay dirt!

*(She presents a package of crumpets to the audience.)*

Ta da! Crumpets! We used to always have them for special occasions, like birthdays or Christmas. Delicious—

*(She pulls out a toaster and plugs it in.)*

—toasted! Nobody knows I have this! I have to be careful when I use it because of the smell... And they'll have to have butter, dripping off them.

*(She pulls out some margarine.)*

I use this because it's cheaper—and sugar, and cinnamon! It's like a fresh, hot, cinnamon bun! I love cinnamon buns. I have a cinnamon bun!

*(She digs out a half-eaten cinnamon bun from her bag of leftovers.)*

Oh—and since this is "The Last Time," I'll have to have my favourite!

*(She gets out a bag of icing sugar.)*

Icing!

*(AMANDA finds a bowl and a spoon and begins to cream the icing sugar with the margarine.)*

If Mom ever made a cake, my sister and I used to wait around for the beaters to lick. I'd lick each metal spoke over and over but I never seemed to get enough.

*(She casually gets some milk from the back of the toilet or another hidden spot.)*

Now I never let myself touch the stuff because I know it will turn into instant fat.

*(She quietly mixes up the icing for a minute and then looks around for something to nibble on.)*

When I am busy getting stuff ready, I like to have a little something to tide me over.

*(AMANDA continues to look around the table of food and stops at the bread.)*

Sugar and butter on white bread is perfect—because it's fast...

*(She butters and sugars a piece of bread and takes a bite.)*

...and delicious. Or cookies! Cookies are great tide-me-overs!

*(AMANDA finds a bag of cookies.)*

You can open them up on the way back from the store.

*(She opens them and spreads a few on the table.)*

They're getting expensive though. But sometimes you can find rolls of cheap Danish ones in the drug store.

I go shopping a lot. Sometimes to quickly replace the food I've eaten from the cupboards—or sometimes for direct supplies. It gets expensive! I bet I spend...

*(She pauses to calculate.)*

...over a hundred dollars a week. I spend all my clothing allowance, any money I get from baby-sitting—I've even spent most of the money I got from my Grandmother. And it gets embarrassing when I have to unload it all, in front of everyone, at the checkout! I usually go to different corner stores so nobody will remember me, and I'll make up stories like—that I work at a daycare and we're having a birthday party or something. And I always ask for paper bags. I hate using plastic because if I accidentally meet someone they might see what's inside.

*(AMANDA takes the bread and spreads each piece with icing, making a stack of six to eight slices.)*

For a binge that I have lots of time for, I like to get a huge pile of stuff ready so I can plow into it non-stop.

*(She finishes.)*

There.

*(She picks up the stack and shows it to the audience.)*

This isn't much at all! Usually I can eat three times this amount, but today, for my last time, I get variety—

*(AMANDA puts down the bread and goes to get something else.)*

—like, why not,—taco chips! They are hard to bring back up though, they come up in big lumps…but what helps that is popcorn! It sort of gathers everything else up on it's way out.

*(AMANDA surveys the feast and remembers one last thing.)*

Crumpets!

*(The crumpets have popped out of the toaster. AMANDA lathers them with butter, cinnamon and icing sugar. She takes a delicious and most satisfying bite. She looks out at the audience and enjoys the crumpet with them. She takes another bite but gradually becomes painfully aware of the audience staring at her. She surveys the food table and tries to take another bite of the crumpet. She stops. The grossness, the strangeness, and the shamefulness of what she is doing, in front of them all, hits home to her. She can not eat any more.)*

*(AMANDA quietly tries to explain.)*

I don't know why I do this. I don't know… I mean…this me? This me that's talking to you right now? I would never do that. I mean—I'm sane—I'm intelligent…and I have this great life…and *I* would never waste my time doing that.

*(She pauses to try and figure it all out.)*

It seems like…this other thing possesses me, out of the blue—and I end up doing it—and *this* me, gets smaller and smaller until it almost goes away. But it never actually does. There's always a little part of it left, right back here.

*(She indicates a specific place at the back of her head.)*

And if I look at the world outside, it seems like there is this thick glass or haze separating me from it. Or if I look at people around me, they seem really really far off, like in another space. And while I eat, this tiny part of me watches, and sometimes tries to make me stop, but it's way too small so I just block it out. That way I can finish eating and throw up. Throwing up is the only route back to *this* me.

*(AMANDA looks back at all the food.)*

After the initial relief of deciding to eat and the fun of the first few bites, I usually don't like to think about it too much—or even look at it. So I'll do something else like, I'll watch TV while I eat, or I'll read something.

*(AMANDA glances over at her pile of magazines.)*

In fact, I was eating and reading a magazine when I found out what this whole thing was! I couldn't believe it! Up until then I had honestly thought I was the only one in all the world that would do such a weird thing! I thought I'd been directly reincarnated from the Roman times or something, when they used feathers to tickle their throats! And that's when I found out what it was called "Bulimia." Right away I hated that word.

*(She repeats it distastefully.)*

"Bullliiimia." I still hate it! Why did they have to call it that?

Bul — bul — it sounds like they are making a stupid joke about regurgitating cud — or it sounds like the name of a huge fat cow....

*(She demonstrates.)*

"Bulimia," with these giant udders that flop from side to side — it's ugly, dumb, it sounds fat!

*(AMANDA shudders.)*

I could never imagine going to anyone, not even a counsellor and saying, "I have Bull-iii-mia." That would be so awful.

*(AMANDA sits and continues to tell the audience her story. It is the first time she has talked truthfully and kept no secrets back.)*

I did go to a counsellor — once. I didn't say that "word," but I sort of told her what I did.

*(She lets out a big sigh.)*

I thought she would fix me up and I would walk out of there cured — but she didn't help. I went home and I binged worse than ever! She didn't know much about it and of course I didn't tell her everything, but — you'd think she'd figure it out. I secretly went to my normal doctor too and told her. I thought she'd find some magical medical reason for why I had these cravings, but all she said was to; "simply set my mind to it and quit." The counsellor said that too; "Just quit!" I wish I could! I mean, it makes sense — this is all so stupid there doesn't seem to be any reason why I shouldn't be able to. And I can!

*(AMANDA cheers up as she remembers that this is her last time.)*

Because that is exactly what this is!

*(She indicates the table full of food.)*

This is: "My Big Quit!" The Binge that is going to end all Binges!

*(AMANDA pulls out a cooler.)*

I'd better make sure I use up everything.

*(She gets out a carton of ice cream.)*

Ice cream is great because I love it—and it slides up super easily.

*(She takes a spoonful, savouring it and thinking.)*

You know how I first learned how to do this? I was only in Grade Five and my teacher, Miss Anderson, was giving us our first class in sex education. Well, I suddenly realized that I had never actually seen what a naked guy even looked like, so I went searching—in the school library. I decided to try the medical section hoping a book would have a picture or something. Well, this huge yoga book caught my eye because it had this almost naked man on it's cover, wearing only this little diaper thing, doing all these contortions. I was looking through, hoping I could catch a glimpse up his loin cloth, when I came to this chapter on cleansing. Here he was sitting cross-legged and he had a string going up one nostril and down the other and he was pulling it through to clean his nose! On the next page he had his stomach sucked in to about an inch wide and a little stream of water was pouring out of his mouth! It was called, "Cleansing the Stomach," and it said: "Drink five glasses of warm salt water, blow out all your air, suck your stomach in, and let the water pour out—or, if you must, give a small tickle at the back of the throat with your middle and index finger." Right away this idea popped into my head. I had just found out how fattening ice cream was, so that weekend I collected my allowance, hopped on my bicycle and beetled down to the Dairy Queen. And I bought myself this huge, loaded banana split. I sat right down there on the curb and I gobbled it in, mouthful after delicious mouthful. Then, I got back on my bike and cycled home. Mom and Dad were working and my sister was out so I locked all the doors.

*(AMANDA physically remembers herself back into the story as she tells it.)*

I went into the kitchen and I took down a big beer mug. I filled it with warm water and dumped in tons of salt—then I plugged my nose and glugged it down. And I did it again and again, until I had five of them in my stomach.

*(She remembers how sick she felt.)*

Then I slowly made my way to the bathroom, put the toilet seat up, blew out all my air and pumped in my stomach— nothing happened. So I was about to put my fingers toward my mouth when there was this huge explosion! Warm salty milky water came blasting out of my mouth! And it didn't go into a nice little stream—it went everywhere! All over the floor, into the bathtub, up and over all the walls. And it kept coming—and it kept coming! And it went up and through my nose—and a piece of pineapple got stuck there—and there were bits of strawberries and blueberries and breakfast and— Yuk! I thought it was the grossest thing in all the world! I stopped. And I cleaned it all up, and I thought that I would never, *ever* do that again!

*(AMANDA stops for a moment, bringing herself back to the present.)*

And I never did. Not once! I didn't even think about it again—

*(AMANDA forces herself to face the truth.)*

—until I turned fifteen. Fifteen! I hated fifteen! I was great at fourteen. That's when this picture was taken.

*(AMANDA retrieves a beautiful picture of herself in a bathing suit. She has it somewhere special, perhaps hanging up, as an incentive for her diets.)*

But at fifteen I suddenly started to gain weight! I wasn't eating any more than usual but the pounds seemed to glom on over night! So I immediately started to diet. And at first I did great. I could easily lose five or six pounds in a week. But after awhile I started to gain the pounds back faster than I could lose them. And I began to have these cravings! I mean I'd really crrrraaave—for junky stuff like chocolate and pastry! And the tension would grow and grow until I just broke down and ate. And then I'd hate myself!

So here I was, feeling fat and fifteen, and there was a big school dance coming up. I was on a really strict diet because I was trying to fit into this dress that I had borrowed from my sister, when suddenly, I blew it—and I ate a whole block of cheese melted in the microwave! I got so mad at myself and then—"bang"—I remembered! It was honestly the first time I had even thought about it since Grade Five! I went to the bathroom, and I did that five glasses of water bit, and—well, it was still pretty gross but—

*(AMANDA lets herself feel the relief.)*

—it seemed like magic. And during that year, every now and again, when I was in danger of gaining weight, I would simply go and throw up.

*(As AMANDA continues there is a sense that she is trying to figure all of this out for the first time.)*

But then, the next year, I started doing it not just once every couple of months, but more and more until I was throwing up almost every day! And now? Sometimes I can't stop for weeks! I eat for hours and then I throw up—and I think I'm OK and that I'll go back to my normal life—but then I end up eating for hours again so I have to throw up again.

I'm almost failing in school. I used to get A's and B's but now I am scraping by with C's. I used to never get depressed but lately I can't make it out of bed sometimes and once, at school, the room went totally, literally, black.

*(AMANDA gives a big sigh.)*

I look at all my friends who I should be like, but I can't seem to get back to them…. I wish I was with them now.

*(She stops and takes in where she actually is and looks at all the food on the table. This reminds her that she is working on quitting and she reaffirms her vow:)*

But I will be soon because this *is* my last time of *all* times and then I will be thin and perfect and happy again!

*(AMANDA takes out some leftover Kraft Dinner and*

*eats one or two mouthfuls, mechanically. She is anything but happy as she faces the stark realities of her world.)*

Kraft Dinner is good for when you've eaten too much sweet stuff. There, that's better. Oh, and I can't forget this — *(Presents the next food with a bitter singsong.)...duddle dee du de dah...*

*(She gets out a cake. There isn't any glee left. It's as though she despises the food.)*

A frozen Sara Lee chocolate cake! Oh — and my last time? I can't forget these — *(Singsong.)...duddle dee du de dah!*

*(She gets out a full box of Turtle chocolates. She is very cynical.)*

A whole box of chocolates! I can sit around all afternoon like that Turtle Lady, *(Sings.) "I love Turtles yah yah yah!"*

*(She clicks back to reality.)*

The caramel in them is really hard to get back up though.

*(She goes back to being cynical.)*

But — what helps that is — another treat binge item, Coke!

*(A half-full, two litre bottle of Coke appears.)*

It works even better than water because it erodes everything first.

*(She takes a long drink. It seems to calm her a little as she looks out at the audience and goes on.)*

I must admit, my system is starting to break down. You know that little flap in the back of your throat that opens and closes when you eat? Well, I think mine is broken because I don't need my fingers any more. The food just comes up automatically, even when I don't want it to...and quite often there's blood. And I've managed to wreck my teeth. The dentist told me I had eight thousand dollars worth of work to do on them. Eight thousand dollars! My parents just about died! He explained to them that it could be from a thing called "Bulimia" because the acid in the stomach coming up erodes the teeth, or, he said, it could be hereditary. My parents immediately decided it was hereditary, but I know—and I'm sure the dentist knows, that it was from throwing up so much.

I did tell my parents about this thing. They do know! Right after I read that article I took it to them and I said:

*(AMANDA imagines herself back talking to her parents:)*

"I do this."

*(She points to an imaginary magazine article.)*

"I don't know why. I know, it's *so* stupid. You don't have to worry! I am never going to do it again." They were glad I had talked to them, but then—we've never mentioned it since.

*(AMANDA wonders about this and then comes up with the answer.)*

I guess they really believed me when I said that I could quit!

*(AMANDA gets out a package of red licorice. It is the last thing she has hidden in her room.)*

For some strange reason if the last thing you eat is red licorice, it's also always the last thing that comes out—so you know when your stomach is empty. And I've started to throw up at half-hour intervals so nothing has the chance to turn into fat. Food, toilet—toilet, food—food, toilet—toilet…

*(AMANDA has indicated back and forth between the table and the toilet and finally lets her gaze rest upon the toilet. She surprises herself with her next realization.)*

I know a lot about toilets! I've done major research in different toilets! Can you imagine? I could give you all a lecture on the ideal toilet!

*(AMANDA goes further, becoming a little cynical again.)*

I could stand here, and call myself something like—Ms

Upperchucker, here to talk to you all today about toilets.

*(AMANDA assumes the character of her imagined Ms Upperchucker.)*

"Rule Number One! Scout out a good toilet before starting a binge. You want to find a private one with a solid locking door. Nothing worse than being stuck in a cubicle throwing up and having to listen for other people coming in. But if that happens, then stop, turn your feet around and…"

*(She reverts back to being herself)*

…pretend to blow your nose or something. I've waited in cubicles for hours while someone does their make-up or fixes their hair!

*(She goes back to being the lecturer but it is less pronounced.)*

Or, "Rule Number Two! The best actual toilet is one without too much water in the bowl. That gives you a nice porcelain slide for the procedure.

*(AMANDA does a hand gesture of a slide.)*

A bowl full of water is terribly messy and noisy. But, again, if you're stuck, then flush the toilet, quickly throw-up a few times, then wait, and flush the toilet and throw up again. Or, sometimes there is a small dry space at the back and you can inch your head in there being careful not to touch the dirty lifted seat…."

*(AMANDA has stooped over to demonstrate but stops and goes back to herself as she digests the strangeness of it all. She continues quietly and seriously.)*

My father took so much time teaching his children about proper hygiene for public washrooms. Sometimes, I wonder what he would think if he ever saw my face scrunched up to the toilet seat and covered in puke.

*(She gathers herself to press on.)*

I mean, I know every toilet in my high school — all the ones at my friend's houses — the best ones downtown. I even know lots of toilets around British Columbia — Heck! I know toilets across Canada!

*(AMANDA takes a large beer mug and pours a full glass of water from a pitcher. She dumps in some salt. There is a sense that she is going to next go and throw up.)*

And I can see each one of them. Because once you've been head to head with them, you really know them well.

*(AMANDA gulps down the water. She settles in to tell a final story. As she recounts the story she puts herself more and more into it so by the end it is as though she is there.)*

Like this one toilet in Toronto. I'll never forget that toilet. I was there with my parents but they had dropped me off at a movie by myself. Half-way through this weird thing happened. I began to see all these amazing pastries that we had passed on the way to the theatre. So I got up — left — and found myself back at the bakery. The next thing I knew I was sitting on this park bench, surrounded by all these gooey cakes that I was gobbling up. And suddenly I felt really really full. Only I had forgotten to do that number one rule. Find a good bathroom first. So I began searching, feeling sicker and sicker — and I couldn't find one anywhere. Finally — I was directed to this one down a long, dark, dead-end alley. I knew I was not in the safest part of Toronto, but I also knew I had to go down there. So I did.

*(AMANDA physically goes down the imaginary alley and into the bathroom.)*

And at the end was this tiny bathroom — and you go in — and — it was so filthy. You could smell the urine — there was this big pile of shit in the corner — the sink was covered in guck — and there was brown smeared all over the toilet, no toilet paper — nothing. But I knew I had to do it, only, I had also forgotten to drink anything.... So I had to get some water out of that sink —

*(She remembers back to how difficult and disgusting this was.)*

—and I did. I drank some water—and I threw-up. And I drank more water, and I threw up. And I did it again and again until I was completely empty—finished. "A New Beginning." And I was never going to do that again! So, I got out of there—

*(She leaves the area of her imagined bathroom.)*

—and I was walking back down the alley when this man statred coming towards me, staring at me. I tried to pass him but he grabbed me and rammed himself against me. I hit— and I managed to get away—but I didn't have anywhere to go except back in here.

*(AMANDA has gone back into her imagined bathroom.)*

So I locked the door and he banged and yelled all this crude stuff…. Then everything went quiet, and I waited—trapped in this horrible, stinking bathroom that I had just thrown up in. And then there was this rustling outside—and under the door came these grossest, most violent, pornographic pictures—using all these little kids…. And they kept coming, and they kept coming, and all I could think of was that this was all my fault! I had put myself here, in this bathroom, to throw up. And I vowed right then that I would never, ever do this again—throw-up again.

*(AMANDA stops and lets herself slowly come back to the present. She takes a look at the toilet, her bedroom, and all the food laid out and faces the stark reality that if the Toronto episode had not made her quit, this probably wouldn't be her last time either.)*

That was two years ago. I've thrown up hundreds of times since then.

*(She goes over to the food on the table and questions herself.)*

My last time? "My Last Ever In My Whole Life Binge"? Somehow—I don't think so. I think I need to find help.

*(She touches her grandmother's ring, still on her finger.)*

"White Rabbits, White Rabbits, White Rabbits…."

*(She looks out at the audience.)*

Please, help—me.

*(AMANDA takes one last look at all the uneaten food, then she slowly turns and, determined, exits from her room.*

*The End.)*

# Afterword

I would like to say a few words about my own recovery from bulimia. I had always thought it would be a momentous occasion to be celebrated year after year: "The Day I Beat the Big B!" But it didn't work out that way at all. It was fourteen years ago that I, like Amanda at the end of the play, knew I had a serious problem and set forth to solve it, but when did I actually stop being bulimic? There is no exact date. At first I'd go three days without throwing up, then a week, then a month, then two months! Then, just as I thought my struggles were behind me, I'd slip up again. The path to success was a gradual process that lasted about six years.

I had also thought that I would find one magic cure or answer to my problem. In the search for this answer I read many books on self awareness, on diets, and on health and eating disorders. My reading made me realize that instead of having just the problem of throwing up, I had many blocked areas to examine and release. From the books, I learned valuable exercises which I did religiously in the hope of emerging from my dark tunnel and, gradually, I began to see glimmers of light through the process. Each book was a step that brought me closer to freedom.

Along with my books I went to several counsellors, but I never lasted more than a few visits. Looking back, I realize that it would have helped to keep looking for a professional counsellor with whom I felt truly comfortable. My parents did try to help me through my roughest periods but I was never truly honest with them at the time and did not allow them to know that I was still very much bulimic after telling them I had improved.

One of the strongest driving forces behind my recovery was the support of a close friend. I checked in with her regularly and honestly through many years, sharing my triumphs, my defeats, my slip ups and my discoveries. We spent a fortune on champagne which we would "pop off" to cheer me onwards after my discouraging set backs. It was this constant "checking-in" that kept me in touch with reality and helped me to continue towards a healthier life style.

However, am I completely recovered? A few years ago I didn't think complete recovery was possible. Though I no longer threw up, I thought I'd always be afraid of food, afraid of getting fat, afraid of "The Big Binge." I was constantly on a diet and constantly weighing myself. I felt depressed when the scales went up and happy when they went down. I fasted for days if I was acting in a play and my costumes were revealing ones, and I dreaded the fittings, afraid I may have gained weight since my measurements were taken. I would look at the beautiful women in the dressing room and wish their slim waists, or thin legs, or sleek arms upon me. It was not until recently, when I was writing my play and again reading books on eating disorders, that I began to see the diet trap that one could get entangled in, and realized that I was snared.

I had never before thought about the long-term implications of dieting, presuming a particular diet was over and done with once the pounds were shed. One theory that fascinated me was that our metabolism still worked as it did thousands of years ago when our food supply was directly dependent upon a successful hunt or upon our crops. After a time of famine, our body would immediately store up extra fat reserves to prepare for any future crisis. Suddenly my neverending, yo-yo weight pattern began to make sense. My metabolism must have thought it was unbelievably bad luck that famine hit me every few weeks! I had always thought that someone was fat because they ate huge desserts and didn't do any exercise when, in reality, they may have dieted the pounds on!

I began to wonder about my obsession to look "slim." Who defined what I "should" look like? Was it me? Or was it our society and an enormous industry of fashion, diet, and make-up? I remembered a passionate paragraph I had written when I was eight, railing against people who judged someone by their looks and not by who they were inside. I wondered when I had first judged myself by my exterior and when I began to judge others by theirs.

In the midst of "weighing" all these questions, I delivered a beautiful, healthy baby boy. And, surprise of all surprises, I did not immediately lose the extra fifty pounds that I had gained! When I went to get dressed I took one look at my tiny pair of pre-pregnancy jeans and I knew I was in trouble. I waited for the panic to set in. Dieting was out of the question since I did not want to jeopardize the baby's health. What could I do? I decided that for the first time in my adult life, I would not worry about my poundage: I would let my body weight adjust itself naturally. I was amazed at how relieved I was by this decision, and surprised that my days were just as alive and fun as when I was slim. My weight took about eight months to adjust itself to twenty pounds more than I'd ever before allowed myself to weigh. Again, I was astonished to discover that I did not mind. I felt healthy and even beautiful! I began to look at people around me and instead of criticizing their body shape, marvel at how unique and extraordinary we each are.

Am I completely recovered today? Sometimes, if I take a second dessert, I expect screaming voices to plunge me into anxiety and despair, but I can thankfully say that they have completely disappeared. My weight no longer dictates to me who I am and how I should feel. I am free. It is the first true freedom I have experienced since childhood.

# A Prop Note

There is a certain prop in the play that is meaningful to me as a performer, but that the audience does not get to fully experience. It is Amanda's diary and the pages she rips out. With the fear that it may be indulgent to reveal such raw material, I'd like to include some selected, unedited entries from my own personal journals. I don't have any from my very sick days. Like Amanda, I threw them all out, but I did find some scattered entries in journals I kept during the years I was trying to recover.

# Diary of a Bulimic

May 31st, 1980

Strange—me? How did this all happen—why? I understand more about the losing of a precious hour, day, week, month. The month of May. In my worst hours, when my poor tummy is stuffed and my head is sore and reeling, I am still in the background. A small tiny voice in the back of my neck, waiting to be set free.

I hope the time has come. I feel I have experienced and learned more than I ever would have, had I stayed sane, but I think the time has come to file the experience and get on with my life—so maybe this time it will happen.

So I close another month. I believe one can do anything that they really want. I can too. I've succumbed enough to know that I want to be set free. So, I swear, as of this hour, I shall try.

June 1st, 1980

Who—me? What? Made it through one super day? Holy Smokes! I am afraid of the overpowering need for a binge that may come over me still tonight. I've never been in jail. I've always been free to take the dive down. But the feeling when I am on a binge of having to know where the next junk food is going to come from while still swallowing my tenth chocolate bar—makes me think that an addict in jail must go through hell. But I made it through today.

June 2nd, Midnight, 1980

I'm disgusted, fed up, ready to throw my life away. But then that is what I've been doing for the past months anyway. Only Day Two and I'm crying again.

June 10th, 1980

I'm no farther ahead. It seems I've listed my priorities so many times — only to forget them at the crucial moment. From this moment I can only try once more and say good riddance to chocolate, sugar, and chemicals and hello to me. I swear by my true self, me, that I will.

June 14th, 1980

I remember my loneliness of Valentine's Day. There was a gentle breeze and though I had plugged my body, the breeze breathed a fresh hope. This evening, once again, I feel that breeze and write through my experience upon the subject of my habit in the hope of figuring it out.

The cycle begins with withdrawal. The mind and body feel sick and cry out forcefully for relief. Motives are warped. Freedom means a place to black out the world and binge.

Stage two is eating. I tell myself that a mouthful is all I need, but deep inside I know that once I've begun, I won't be able to stop.

The final stage is the most pleasant one, providing the stomach is not too stretched so pain masks the mind's relief. It is from this final stage that I now write. I make plans for tomorrow. Since I have put myself near the bottom of my despair hole I have something to strive for, a place to climb to. I can plan: "Tomorrow I will fast."

Meanwhile, deep inside, I know I shall have to contend with the beginning of the cycle again tomorrow. I have been at this long enough to know I am in trouble. I have said, "this is the last time" enough to know the chances of it really being the last time are slim. For three weeks I've been trapped and I can feel myself being wheeled toward destruction where I won't be able to return. Many times in stage two I've thought of how useless and undesirable is the life I am leading. I know it is dangerous. If only the tears of regret that come near the end of stage two could be moved to stage one. I am better not eating at all. Actually feel quite good after a few days like that, but I can not abstain forever from food like alcohol or drugs. How can I think so clearly and yet be so screwed up!

November 3rd, 1981

I am determined to become a healthy soul and body before this diary turns into another year! I shall listen to my body from inside, as I have been

learning to do, and unravel the bottom of this iceberg. I will write when-
ever I want to get out the thoughts and feelings that may otherwise lead to
the habit of hell.

1:35 p.m. My head is sore. The mind thinks of ways to make me feel
better, like sugar food. Mucky is my head. I think I'll walk. I feel at a loss
for things to do but I know there are things out there.

10:35 p.m. I get my sticker for an accomplished non-heave-up day!

November 4th, 1981

Whew, it seems ages since I started this diary, yesterday. My head
is full, but not grumpy, just not too bright. My body is all plugged up. I
know I ate too much last night, by the scale I gained three pounds. I am
afraid of getting fat, but what is that compared to the hell life of the habit?
I did everything on my list and I feel good. My, I build, create and carry a
lot of tension!

November 5th, 1981

Now I woke up feeling quite bright this morning and proud of
myself for having such a wonderful day before!

12:07 I am at this moment on the verge of an upset. I thought I'd go
swimming at 11:30. I decided I didn't want to. My head began to feel at
loose ends. I ate a banana, then still feeling frustration went on eating rice
and salad. A small voice saying, "Watch out, you won't be able to stop."
Another voice yelling, "Go for it and get rid of it!" I will lie down and get
up and have my proper lunch I planned. Seems easy. All so sensible. But
it is so hard!

November 6th, 1981

I am proud, proud, proud of myself!

November 16th, 1981

My weight is doing strange and wonderful things! I'm used to it
bouncing way up unless I keep control of it through Bulimia—but this
week it has kept pretty steady! Even when I woke up like this morning and
thought—"Oh no! I'm going to have to starve for awhile, the scales are

going to register a ton" — they don't, making me quite gleeful.

November 17th, 1981

I love this "Diary of a Bulimic." I must say it helps me so much.

December 1st, 1981

I don't believe it! I am on the verge of throwing up!! I've already eaten more than is good for me and just hummed through the fridge wondering what I could gobble!

December 2nd, 1981

Whew! Yesterday I came closer to binging than I have for a long long time!

December 7th, 1981

Ahhhhhhhhhhhhhhhh! I did it AGAIN!!!!!
The pressure built,
My unhealth grew,
the day went on,
but my clear thought flew — away.

I tried to grasp,
I tried to hold,
But something snapped,
and I started to fold,
I ate one, two, four things,
And then took the dive:
Into the gray land,
where I cease to exist,
My self deeply covered,
In piles of mist.

Hours cruise by,
each more painful than the last,
until I purge to deep bottom
And sink to the past.

And here slowly stroke upward,
And gasp in new air,
And strike out again,
to myself try to be fair.
Which brings me to now,
as tired, depleted, I write,
I hang to hope—from now on
My struggles will direct me alright.
Whewwwwwwwww.

January 20th, 1982

It seems like a year since I last was on the surface of life, cruising along in my sail boat.

On December 7th, 1981 my boat rocked over and I took on some water. I bailed that out but then for the rest of the month I had around ten more spills. It seemed I'd almost get my ship sailing on path again but I'd oversee or neglect some maintenance work and over I'd go! I did manage to steer my ship safely into Christmas Week and had a wonderful and successful time then.

However, the first two weeks in January brought a major upset. My ship went over on January 4th and I have been floundering in the stormy seas since! I did have various days that I surfaced to keep my breath and life but I never got the bailing done. This brings me to today. It is pouring with rain outside. Had a lovely silent walk. I have a glimpse, for the first time ever, of my potential as a human being and life force. This glimpse gives me a reason to strive forward and grab onto that potential and sail with it. Like harnessing the winds. Like focus. Today I will begin again sorting out, clearing out, and tidying up my ship.

January 28th, 1982

I have a sense inside of me,
Of what that me can possibly be.
Out there in the world where everything's busy,
I now can survive without getting dizzy.
I can keep my joy of life all safe,
My security and visions live through the fast pace.
To love one's self is to love the world,
And to love the world—in all it's turmoil,
Is Freedom.

February 4th, 1982

I feel tired and like a slug. Yesterday I overfed. Some is still with me today. "Heellpp!" It is my birthday tomorrow. It was my "be beautiful" deadline. I see now that is warped. I am a beauty now, yesterday and today. I try to remember the wonderful feelings when I was young. It is natural I make eating mistakes. I am discovering and learning. I am making my way out of the labyrinth I constructed in my mind these past twenty years, clearing paths behind me to go ahead. Today I shall breathe deeply. Thanks Diary.

February 7th, 1982

Feeling wonderful. (My head keeps saying I am fat. I'll just yell back three times "wonderful, wonderful, wonderful!") Now where was I—ah yes, on my way out the door....

February 8th, 1982

I thought, as I ate another frozen cookie: "I'd rather be doing something else." In the old days I was wanting to avoid the "something else's," or I was in such a pit of despair I wanted to escape. Not yesterday. Yes, I blew it, but I think I am going onward—somehow—still.

July 1st, 1982

A new part of my book. A new chapter, so to speak. I always expected the world and my life to be rosy, wonderful and perfect, especially once I quit my bad habit, but that world is impossible. I quit my habit but my life was not great, pressure built, worry mounted, and life sometimes seemed no easier than when I binged. My perception of the wonderful world has to change. Yes, it does. If I fall, I can cry and still have fulfilling moments, but if I criticize or blame regarding the fall or worry about the next—"POW" there goes the easy flow. Here comes the binge. I am changing, slowly but surely.

November 7th, 1982

Well—it has been five months!! I can hardly believe it!

November 12th, 1982

Whoopee! Another star day on my calendar!

November 17th, 1982

A star day! It was a toughie though. Lot's of "you're fat," "worthless," "can't stand this," "can't stand that," thoughts going round my head.

December 17th, 1982

It is so hard writing my "Success Journal" after a set-back! It has taken me until eight-thirty the following night to begin. But I must remember that the day had success even through the upset.

December 31st, 1982

New Year's Resolutions are popping into my mind. This is a huge step. For years I've not been able to make any as the one big problem was impossible to conquer. Now I see it disappearing behind me.

March 11th, 1983

I did wonderfully—until February this year! I made my first slip up then—sllllide to old habit! Like a first cigarette it turned into ten. Ten times. Or less. But there. I have to catch hold of some ground. Breathe. Release. Let go to travel onward.

April 12th, 1983

I just wrote a cold turkey vow. I can't believe how fast I can slide into a nightmare world of depression, despair, avoidance, denial of me, just like the olden days.

I know I must trust the new me deep inside who is beginning to emerge, know I have not killed it but just need to open some windows and let the sun in again.

June 19th, 1983

Too many slip ups!!! And I hate, yes, hate what they do to me—my tongue, my teeth, my head. I struggle onward.

January, 1984

My little diary. You are full of me. My pains, my mix-ups, my me-
ness. When storms come up I must remember that it is my perception of
the adventures of these storms that will sail me through them. Champagne
on a rainy afternoon day off, by myself, to celebrate my six months of
clean living behind me and to toast the adventures ahead. Bon Courage,
Bon Chance.